An Account of a Walk on the Chesil Beach

by John P.Kemp

Drawings by: Judy Palmer, Trevor Price, Nigel Clarke

GW00658930

Nigel J. Clarke Publications
Unit 2, Russell House,
Lym Close, Lyme Regis,
Dorset. DT7 3DE
Tel: 01297 442513
Fax: 01297 442513

Web site www.njcpublications.demon.co.uk
e-mail nigel@njcpublications.demon.co.uk

ISBN 0 907683 18 5

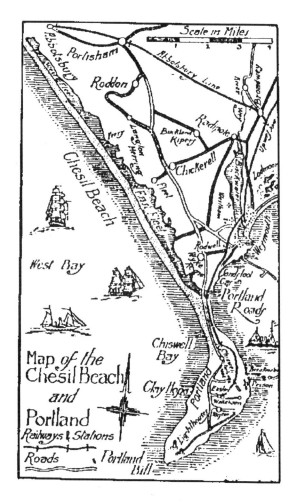

Map of the Chesil Beach and Portland

Railways & Stations

Roads

INTRODUCTION

The Isle of Portland, a Royal Manor, scarcely makes it as an island. Below the bridge at Ferrybridge, which makes a direct road link, the water which ebbs and flows would, if it met the sea on the other side of the bridge, make it truly an island. Instead it turns sharp right and forms a brackish mere - called the Fleet - about 9 miles long, bounded on the seaward side by the Chesil Beach, and ends at Abbotsbury, where the beach very definitely joins the land.

4

THE CHESIL

The Chesil (from Old English meaning stones) can best be seen in its entirety from the War Memorial above Fortuneswell on Portland. It curves South East/North West, a finely curved blade with continual surf along its length. From where it starts at Portland, elegantly joined to the jumble of cliffs and stones and the new sea wall, it continues with a decreasing size of stones to end at Eype's Mouth, 22 miles away.

"EMMA MARIA"
Wrecked on 25th October, 1903' Chesil Beach.

Here, at Chesil Cove, more wrecks have occurred than in most of the British Isles; ships failing to round the Bill in an onshore gale stood little chance of beating out. You will see no remains. The relentless grinding of the beach and the predations of beachcombers have seen to that. In addition, strong currents tended to carry the pathetic remains of other wrecks which took place further along the beach to this sad place.

The sea defences were completed in 1983, and the concrete ramparts seem impregnable. But an Islander, eyes red with a lifetime's work in the quarries, spoke scornfully of them. "Nothing" he said "ever stops the sea from coming in if it has a mind to."

Chesilton itself, behind the wall, is a mixture of bright homes and empty hovels, abandoned shops and a windswept cleanliness. It has suffered many floods, and despite the new defences is redolent with an air of insecurity.

Crunching on towards Ferrybridge from Portland, the beach is at its widest point. At Small Mouth, the exit and entry of the Fleet to and from the open sea, there used to be a ferry from the causeway to the mainland. In the Great Storm of 1824, the ferry house was swept away; the ferryman was also lost, while attempting to save a soldier.

The ferry had been rope guided, whilst at low tide horses and carts could ford their way across. The bridge was built in 1839, and has been improved upon ever since. It carries a great deal of traffic to and fro; stone that was used in the building of St.Paul's and the Cenotaph ,and the extra burden of traffic to and from the old air station.

PETRORILIA (Belgian barque)
Grounded on the Chesil Beach 9th December, 1856

There is as yet little plant life on the beach; the stones are too large to hold humus and nutrients, but it seems to contain a mass of small spiders.

In the 1630s an attempt was made to dam the Fleet at Small Mouth, to reclaim the land beneath the waters of the Fleet, but the seeps through the Chesil beach was too great and the project was abandoned. Some few men do still make a living here from fishing for bass, mullet and flounders, etc., but stocks seem to be diminishing.

As elsewhere on the South Coast, this area played an important part in the Normandy Landings, being a marshalling area for vehicles.

In many respects this is the most interesting part of the beach, visually at least. It is very wide, and labouring down from the top of the bank to the shores of the Fleet, and away from the perpetual growl of the sea, the walking becomes easier. The ground is more compact with patches of vegetation making oases among the stones, - tufts of cotton grass, withered now in the winter, and even a bloom on a sea campion plant.

On the shore of the Fleet, dead eel grass forms an endless carpet, the water is clear, with here and there a sheet of sea lettuce wrinkling in the winter sun.

In this lower part of the Fleet, fairly close to Smallmouth, the water is quite saline, but the further one goes into the fastness of the Fleet, the less saline it becomes; this makes for a wide variety of aquatic life.

6

DRAWING OF DORSET LERRET

A lerret was the traditional boat along this coast, some built to carry four oars, some six. They were double-leretenders, pointed at bow and stern, and were first recorded in the 17th century. Only in recent times have they disappeared but there is a fine example in Weymouth Museum. They were probably last built before the last war.

The Fleet here is quite deep, and there are many quite large boats at moorings. Some have resident cormorants as caretakers, making their mark. A small boat piled with crab pots putters up the Fleet, and a few Oyster Catchers on hivering wings quest along the shore.

There are innumerable small dinghies rotting away, split like herring and far beyond repair, and there are possibly more dinghies which are in use from time to time, all scattered above the tide line. or huddled close to tarred sheds and boathouses. But of a lerret, no sign.

Struggling up the beach again, one realises the heavy labour in dragging boats and gear up the beach, then down again. Horses (known as dorsers) were much used; it was a tough job nevertheless, heaving heavy gear 30ft up the shingle, followed by the steep descent to the sea. The horses carried panniers, into which the catch would be loaded, taken back to the village and divided, and any surplus carried inland to be sold.

In time, powered winches, placed at the top of the beach, were used to haul the boats and gear up the slope, and to brake them as they began their descent. Occasionally one comes across the rusted remains.

A slight change of tone and feeling underfoot makes us pause for a moment; there is a vaguely hollow sound, a feeling of insecurity. Beneath our feet, showing only as a slight declivity, a sort of dent in the beach, is a seepage 'can', an area of beach more porous than the rest where the sea filters through into the Fleet. In fact, the Fleet largely depends on this seepage, as there are no feeder streams from the land to have much impact on the volume of water in the Fleet. It is scarcely surprising that the effort to reclaim the Fleet in 1630s was doomed to fail.

We make our way to the summit of the beach once more, and again are surprised at its immensity. It seems hours since Portland was left behind, yet there it is, large and still at our heels. We who walk on it feel very insignificant.

On the seaward side the beach falls in two stages to the sea, two steep slopes each falling about 15ft onto a narrow 'terrace'. On the Fleet and landward side the slope is far less.

On a calm day it is hard to imagine the kind of weather that could lift a ship not merely onto the beach but over it. But in 1839 a 500 tonner was cast so far over the great crest of the beach that it was easier to re-float her on the Fleet. It played similar tricks in the Great Storm of 1824.

THE LIGHTHOUSE, *Portland Bill*

A WINDOW ON THE ATLANTIC

So where does this great power come from, this power that can scoop 4 million tons of stone away and then replace it within a matter of days? The answer lies in the fact that the beach faces a 'window' to the Atlantic. A straight line SW would meet Venezuela, a line broken only by an island or two in the Azores; there is a lot of sea leaning on the beach, and a few thousand miles for it to get going!

The stones that comprise the beach drift from West to East, the larger ones moving the furthest until brought to a halt by Portland; they may well have their origin in the sunken beach which lies between Portland and Start Point. The beach has been accurately dated; 4000 years ago the entire area was swampy, and borings have shown that pine and alder grew on the higher ground.

Another theory, probably more tenable, attributes the stones as being of glacial shaping. When the last Ice Age retreated about 20,000 years ago, the sea rose again, and the general West/East currents brought back the stones that the Ice Age had taken further out.

Among these millions of stones some are found with holes right through them. They were called lucky stones, as elsewhere, and also as hag stones and witch stones. Such stones were carried as charms in every boat. They are not easy to find!

The strangest finds on the more remote parts of the beach are shoes! At an average of every eighty steps one comes across a shoe, and they are most extraordinary shoes. They are huge, ugly, and never in pairs, and one feels that they must come from some strange, single footed race not yet known to man.

There is a vast string of flotsam and jetsam all along the beach; much of it is plastic, beginning to fracture and break up, and the writing on them,

Newspaper illustration of the wreck of the Catherine on Chesil Beach in 1795

if decipherable, is usually continental. The main culprit of this sort of rubbish is shipping, although fishermen and tourists play their part in adding to it with enthusiasm. Of greater interest was the find of the complete cartilage skeleton of an angler fish, every particle of a beautiful curve.

Ship wrecks produced a wonderful bounty, and there were those who were not above setting false lights to lure a ship to its doom. When the Royal Adelaide was wrecked in 1872, carrying emigrants, mayhem followed the washing ashore of belongings of every imaginable kind. Looters swarmed to the scene, while the survivors - only 4 were lost - could only look on in horror.

Some of those who found casks of liquor died of alcoholic poisoning or died of exposure through lying drunk on the beach. Fights were bloody and frequent; and at the end nothing was left. Nothing, that is, except for a little portable sewing machine now on display in Weymouth Museum, rather poignant testimony.

The wreck occurred off Wyke Regis, where the church is a prominent point for ships approaching Portland, and whose churchyards, two of them, are full of those unfortunates who perished in the sea.

In World War II a Tank Landing Craft was wrecked, with the loss of twelve lives.

THE NARROWS

Now we are approaching the Narrows, and an ebb tide flows fast. Between the beach and the shore, weaving among buoys, Army Bridge Laying Craft are practising their skills. From the huge concrete ramp on the further side, Officers and NCOs shout through loud hailers giving hearty encouragement in a language of short barks and short words. Against the current, unladen boats, flat and squat, are planing, weaving white seams across the current. Then,

The Paddle Steamer "BOURNEMOUTH"
1886

turning to run with the current they race away to turn back again just ahead of the safety boats, keeping station where the Narrows widen.

We have by now travelled about four miles, and there is a definite feeling of leaving the world behind. Soon we come to a line of posts on which notices declare that ahead of us is a Grade 1 Site of Special Scientific Interest. As though to emphasise the point, two hares run ahead of us along the beach, a sparrow hawk skims along the contours of the banks, and on the calm waters of the Fleet a black swan swims, weed dangling from its beak. This part of the Fleet permits licensed and restricted shooting.

The Fleet was once a marvellous larder for the villages and hamlets bordering it, and punt guns were frequently used. The punt, rather like a flat bottomed canoe, carried a gun with a bore of an inch or more, and the gunner, lying in the bottom of the punt and usually festooned with greenery to break the outline, would paddle like a ghost towards any large flock of birds. Once he had fired,

and the smoke and chaos had died away, the
water would be strewn with a wide variety of
dead and dying birds, and the onset of a cold
winter had some of the sting taken out of it;
there is nothing like a well stocked larder to set
the mind at rest.

Equally unpleasant things were in store
for the birds - summer visitors; small boys would make traps out of stone and
string, and set them for the wheatears - 100 years ago they would sell for three
pence a dozen.

THE CHESIL AT WAR

There still can be heard the sound of gunfire at Tidmoor Point, where there is
a MOD firing range. The South West Coastal Path runs through the range,
and so presumably does the hiker; but there are red flags when firing is taking
place, and there is no danger. Keeping, for the moment, to the subject of guns,
there was a particularly fierce air battle over Portland in August, 1940, in
which 175 enemy aircraft were involved. Thirty three of them were shot down,
nine by local batteries.

In a derelict dinghy at Tidmoor Point we saw a mass of aluminium
fragments, debris collected from dead planes and a distant war. Weymouth
was also badly bombed in the war. Certainly along the beach and in the hills
behind, there are frequent reminders of that conflict. On the beach tank traps
and pill boxes and gun emplacements are always somewhere to be seen, most
of them sagging into the restless stones, broken beyond recognition; so much
so that they very quickly become part of the landscape. On the premise that
the enemy might make an assault on this stretch of coast, the beach was
heavily mined, and was very definitely out of bounds. But what a lonely patrol

THE CHESIL BANK -
Viewed from the top of Portland

11

for the sentries it must have been, trudging along on duck boards, always with the sea groaning and crashing.

The connection of the beach with war and violence has a long history. The inhabitants of Maiden Castle near Dorchester, a unique prehistoric settlement, used sling stones gathered from the beach before the Romans came.

THE VILLAGE OF FLEET

By now we have reached a point opposite the ancient village of Fleet, and we encounter the year 1824 again, the Great Storm. The beach was breached , and huge seas pounded in and destroyed the church and all but two cottages.

This hamlet should be visited, and the width of the Fleet gauged, and the height of the beach beyond observed. It just does not seem possible that such massive natural defences could possibly fail.

Dead starfish litter the beach. Their numbers in Lyme Bay have grown vastly in recent years, and they have been blamed for the decline in fish stocks; this may be so, but more likely it has been over-fishing, the tearing up of spawning beds, and general changes in

fish population which occur quite naturally. But there are still plenty of fine fish to be caught from the shore, and a number of boats based in West Bay, further down the coast, offer fishermen the chance of deep sea fishing. Some unusual fish have been recorded over the years - blue shark, electric ray, tunney, sun fish, lump fish, boar fish and monk fish. But most anglers are quite content with mackerel, dabs,flounders, whiting, and so on. There are several good local guide books aimed at the angler, so it cannot be as bad as rumours suggest.

The beach is surprisingly free from tar and oil pollution, but strange containers are sometimes washed ashore, and notices go out to warn people off. Away from the more easily accessible parts of the beach, one could collect timber enough to build a house. The really heavy stuff, baulks of timber, huge poles and so on are not easily retrieved, but for the type of person who is interested in 'objets trouve' there are some wonderful sea-wrought items. Occasionally a chunk of blackish shale might be found; this is likely to be Kimmeridge clay, which, together with Oxford clay and Corallim clay, form the foundation on which the beach has grown.

In 1757 a very odd discovery was made; a mermaid had been swept onto the shore. However, reference to its large size, huge nostrils and coarse red hair should have made even the most hopeful think twice, even in those superstitious days. It turned out to be a very dead camel!

Not infrequently finds of a more rewarding sort are made. Gold has been found, both in ingots and coinage form, silver ingots, rings and plates. Pieces of eight are not a rarity, nor is the finding of silver of all ages. After a severe storm metal detectors come out of their cupboards and people, shape

PORTLAND AND CHESIL SEA DOGS
- *these were dogs specially bred to be used in the recovery of barrels of contraband spirits, sunk just off shore, but they are also said to have saved many shipwrecked victims by swimming out and bringing ropes ashore.*

less in their waterproofs eagerly detect. So many ships have foundered all along this shore that there is no doubt that much lies on the sea bed. But before you get out your shovel, the dense clay base on which the beach rests on is some 50ft below high water mark. Riches of another kind have crossed the beach. All the villages lying in their relative safety zone behind the Fleet were deeply involved in smuggling, and goods would be passed from some foreign boat to one or more belonging to the villages, and then taken ashore under the cover of night. Often enough the goods - brandy, lace, tobacco - would have to be sunk, well wrapped and cunningly buoyed, in the Fleet, and then collected and moved on when the coast was clear of Excise men or their informers. The risks were high, and so were the rewards of success; but there are not many good hives (landing places) on the Fleet, roads were no more than heavily rutted bridle tracks, and perhaps a narrow causeway across flooded fields. The chance of ambush was high, and those not involved would indeed 'face the wall while the gentlemen ride by.'

The feeling of remoteness out here is very strong, and the scenery increasingly attractive. The Fleet is dotted with birds; wigeon, teal, red breasted merganser and a long list of birds on passage to faraway places. Moorhen far off are noisily involved in some domestic squabble which so often seems to occupy their energies.

With surprise, so hypnotic is the trudge along the beach, we suddenly notice how much more vegetation there is. By now the stones are beginning to diminish in size, more humus is caught and held, and all forms of life feel the benefit. We can nibble at sea kale (though the root is nicer) despite its withering at the onset of winter. We can still find sea campion, the collapsed and soggy form of the yellow horned poppy - the sap of which was used to heal bruises, and the little black seeds in those shrubby plants must be sea blite, common here but more at home in the Mediterranean. This shrub in particular is invaluable in stabilising the shingle.

In the spring and summer the beach is patched with colour; yellow poppies, herb robert, cranesbill, hawkweed, sea mayweed, ragwort, and the ubiquitous thrift.

RODDEN HIVE POINT TO ABBOTSBURY

Slogging on past Rodden Hive Point, one of many areas rich in fossils, we approach Chipmoor, and the effort of ploughing our furrow is beginning to tell. Oddly enough, there is no lack of moisture among these apparently arid stones; lift one or two and the dampness is very much in evidence. It exists as a result of moist circulating air condensing on the cold underside of the stones. The only thing lacking is humus, but once sea blite has

Kestrel

established its long root systems, it produces and collects more humus for other plants to live on. It is obvious how precarious such a habitat is, and hence the importance of leaving it undisturbed.

This long haul towards Abbotsbury is the most remote and the least disturbed. It is actually an offence to walk the beach in which the Reserve is contained at any time except winter, and even then the walker must keep to the seaward side of the beach so as to avoid upsetting the resting migrant birds on the Fleet. In any case one should seek permission from the Warden of the Stangways estate, to whom it all belongs.

It is in this area that one of the major delights of the beach chooses its breeding ground. The little tern, sometimes called the sea swallow, is quite unadaptable, and will only nest among the sea pea. It is an indescribably beautiful little bird, elegant, eye-catching; one's first glimpse of the bird gives one quite a shock, and constitutes a real thrill for anyone. If you walk the SW Coastal Path you are just as likely to see a mile or so inland, so there is no excuse for trespass. There are also vigilant wardens!

Ringed Plover, known also as stone runners, may be seen, probing and turning stones in its search for sea slaters, woodlouse-like creatures; pied wagtail bob about, looking frail. In due season there are many species of warbler, bunting, wheatear; the problem is that there are so many different species of birds that visit or reside that it is impractical to make a list, but it is worth noting that it is not

necessary to trespass to see many rarities. Ground animals are fewer, but they include voles, mice, shrews ,weasels, and even otters lived here until quite recently.

Passing through another line of tank traps, we reach Abbotsbury, and thankfully we can head for firmer ground and take a rest.

ABBOTSBURY

Abbotsbury has settled at the foot of the downs like an old dog, giving an air of peace and comfort. There are sub-tropical gardens to be visited, the Swannery, the ancient decoy and some wonderful buildings from cottages to the great Tithe barn. It must always have been lovely in one way or another, for all around on the hills and downs Iron and Bronze Age people made this their home, too. One cannot deny ancient man a sense of beauty, but they sited their forts and camps on vantage points which obviously gave them warning of approaching danger, but also provided them with the sort of mixed economy that existed almost to the present day.

MUTE SWANS - *the male is known as a Cob, and can be recognised by the larger fleshy black lump at the base of his beak. The female is called a Pen.*

FISHING - *Seine netting on the Chesil Beach*

From one such point, Chapel Hill, watchmen used to scan the sea for signs of the first mackerel shoals of summer. It was on the shore at Abbotsbury that Defoe in 1724 stated that the mackerel were the largest and finest he had ever seen. At that time they would sell for about a penny a hundred.

The method of fishing left little to chance. The boats, probably lerrets, would be manned and would take out one end of a 400ft net and attempt to encircle a shoal, while the shore gang waited until the encirclement was completed and then they would begin the hauling in. If, despite good fishing by other boats, another was not so successful, they would believe it bewitched, and they would stick pins into a fish, tie it to the rudder and try again.

Traditionally a festival was held on May 13th when garlands of flowers and offerings of beer were rowed out and cast upon the Sea. The intention of course was to placate He who provided the fish, and even today I know some Scotsmen who surreptitiously tip a dram of whisky into the sea before embarking on a trip.

THE GREAT TITHE BARN, *Abbotsbury - The vast building is 270ft long and 30ft wide.*

The beach is about 25ft. high here, and very wide and firm. But in that Great Storm of 1824 the sea burst over the bank and flooded into the village to a depth of 28ft.

From here on the going is very different, the scenery changes, and looking back to distant and misty Portland we can congratulate ourselves. We are half way to our finishing point; and we have a choice. We can be purists and stick doggedly to the stony beach, or we can take a pretty lane which runs beside it. This particular stretch was known as Smugglers Walk, presumably because at last they could actually do just that!

ST.CATHERINE'S CHAPEL, *Abbotsbury. The Chapel built in1461, and dedicated to St.Catherine, the patron saint of unmarried women.*

We pass another concrete block house broken on the beach, and close by is a small terrace of houses and a huddle of tarred boats, nets drying in the sun. With this behind us we now walk along a roughish track, which only really deteriorates once the renovated ex-coastguard house is passed. Shortly after that we come across a notice warning us that vehicles use the track at their own risk, and that the nearest tractor is miles away!

As we scramble onto the beach again, we can notice how much smaller the stones have become, and realise that one can land on the beach in darkness and yet know by the size of the stones roughly where you had landed.

The track is higher than the beach, and is very popular with walkers, and being National Trust property there are no restrictions. Some of the more exotic flowers found on the restricted areas flourish here also, and there is plenty of bird life. There is a general downhill trend to track, and low lying fields hold masses of water in the winter. Marshland flora is much in evidence, but only a narrow strip; the fields are cultivated as close to the beach and track as possible.

ADDER - *shy, and harmless if left alone.*

17

A row of bright little chalets comes into view as we approach West Bexington, an area popular with bird watchers. West Bexington boasts an excellent car park and toilets, and a clean and well kept cafe. This stretch of beach is also popular with anglers, probably due to the proximity of toilets and car park, but good catches have been made here, and many fishing competitions use this as their venue.

Beyond West Bexington, we come to an area of reed beds, cultivated and drained, and warblers may be heard, if not so easily seen here. This is Burton Mere, and demonstrates the likely fate of the rest of the Fleet at some distant date in future. It is known that a far larger area of water existed here once, and it seems likely that the entire beach is slowly rolling over itself to smother the land.

Swyre, on the main road, is not far away, but is completely hidden by small hills, but it can be reached by a path which is more like a causeway than a path. Wet land extends some way inland.

COGDEN BEACH TO WEST BAY

We come onto Cogden Beach, which is wide and fairly level; the footpath dwindles to nothing but stones. Again reeds stretch away in a grey mass, and the hill which rises behind is steep and has a vaguely wilderness look about it. It is one of the nicest areas, for one can be alone and yet can park a car close to the beach, and it has a lovely wild and free feeling about it. But parking is not free, except in the winter, and there is no commercialisation about it. Gravel has been extracted from this part for years, and only ceased in 1984.

THE CHESIL BEACH

From Cogden Beach, where the going is easy as a result of a crumbly but adequate road, we can see ahead to Burton Cliffs, where a caravan site is completely hidden from the beach. To reach Burton Bradstock we have to choose the right state of tide, but many people picnic beneath the cliffs, and there is a car park.

After leaving Burton Cliffs the beach widens again, the cliffs dwindle and we soon reach a lagoon, baulked by the beach. This is the end of the River Bride, which rises some miles away at Bridehead and runs through one of the prettiest of valleys in the county. The road follows this valley, the turning to it being just on the Swyre side of Burton Bradstock and it is well worth exploring.

Burton Bradstock was once a rope making centre, but nearby Bridport took over the industry, by ancient decree, and Burton Bradstock remains a small rural community, popular with tourists and visitors as the large caravan and camping park suggests. It faces the beach, and as we slog on again we pass its frontage.

Eventually the beach narrows again and we reach East Cliff, a towering terrace where layers of Bridport sand and a harder material, Inferior Oolite, have made well used nesting tiers. From the ledges jackdaws and gulls look down impassively on the sweating walker below.

Now we are in West Bay; the cliff, with a golf course on top, is left behind, and as we look inland it is perfectly obvious that we are in an estuary area. Stones have given way to pea gravel, which has been extracted from the beach for years, with apparently no ill effects, and this gravel has travelled to most parts of the world for a variety of uses. Its main use nowadays is in filter beds, and it is shipped out by fairly frequent visits in what is, by West Bay standards, a fairly large ship. The entrance to the harbour is very narrow, and also dependent on the tide, so it is an exciting event when the cargo boat is skilfully brought in, and then turned right round in the restricted waters. The gravel is loaded via a stream of lorries tipping the gravel onto a conveyor belt, which directs it into the hold.

WEST BAY *from East Cliff*

West Bay is a suburb of Bridport, and the river coming from the direction of the town is the River Brit. New sluices and sea defences hold it back, to be released at intervals to scour the little harbour clear of silt. Until the 17th century boats used to sail or be quanted almost into Bridport itself, but in 1740 the harbour proper was built, finally achieving what had been attempted as early as 1388. Once there was a thriving ship building yard, with the last launching being in 1879. The largest ship built was the Speedy, 1002 tons, and a model of it is in Bridport Museum, together with a fascinating display of rope and net making machinery - the industry which has made the town world renowned.

West Bay has a long history of flooding, both from the river and the sea. Huge amounts of money have been spent on sea defences, river drainage, larger sluices, and the completion of these projects came in 1984.

In 1942 the West Pier was breached and a cafe swept away, and in 1974 the little town was inundated, the result of very high tides and gales. All three hostelries were flooded, and the damage to property and boats was enormous. This time the East Beach had been swept away.

On with the last short stage of the walk; having circumnavigated the harbour crowded with fishing boats and a smaller number of private craft, we walk westward along a splendid promenade, one of the new bastions of defence to keep the sea where it belongs. On our right hand side a steep wall of blue lias mud ascends steeply to a row of houses, and always, at the retaining wall, is a new slick of clay. At the end of the promenade we scramble down to the beach over huge imported blocks of Portland stone, and then we meet the stones again. The clay cliffs on our right weep their mud onto the beach, falls are not infrequent, and this is not the most beautiful part of the beach! But its interest for us is that here and there are patches of sand.

It was along this stretch of beach that a large quantity of Roman coins was found in the 1930s; they were assumed to have been part of a hoard finally exposed by the erosion of the cliffs.

At last we are at Eype's Mouth, truly the beginning or end of the greatest shingle banks in Europe. We can rest now, or climb the small cliff steps and look back along the stretch we have walked, and we might well wonder how we made it.

But it was worth it. It has been a good walk.

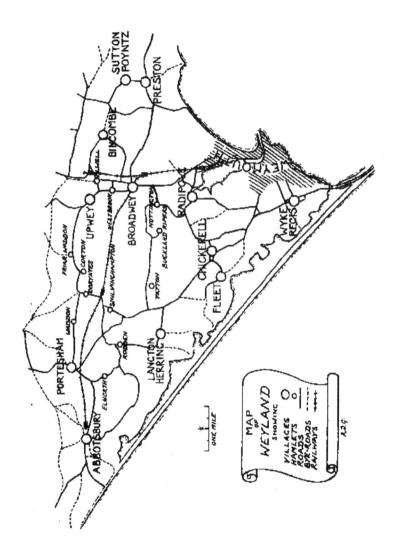

Map of the Chesil drawn in the early 1940's, clearly showing
its relationship to the Fleet and the surrounding countryside.

Other books of local interest are also available:-

WALKING GUIDES:-
West Dorset & East Devon Walks
Dorset & Purbeck Walks
Ten East Dorset Coastal Walks
Ten West Dorset Coastal Walks
Ten East Devon Coastal Walks
Dorset Rubber Stamp Pub Walks

LOCAL INTEREST GUIDE BOOKS:-
The Book of the Cobb, Lyme Regis
Smugglers Tales of Dorset & Devon
Folklore & Witchcraft in Dorset & Wiltshire
The Rude Man of Cerne & Other Wessex Landscape Oddities
Lyme Bay Fossils - a beach guide
The Book of Maiden Castle, Dorchester
The Monmouth Rebellion of 1685
The Heart of Wessex - Exploring Hardy's Dorset
The Book of Weymouth & Portland
Mary Anning - a Brief History
West Country Farmhouse Recipes

We also publish local map guides and tide time tables.
For a full up to date list of all our current publications,
visit our web site at:-
www.njcpublications.demon.co.uk.

Nigel J. Clarke Publications
Unit 2, Russell House,
Lym Close, Lyme Regis,
Dorsct. DT7 3DE
Tel: 01297 442513
Fax: 01297 442513